For our children, Finn, Ava, Jai and Meera.

May your creativity keep you from the clutches of apathy.

And if that fails, at least find a way to get paid for complaining.

APATHETICAL SYDNEY

A PARODY

PAUL CHAPPELL & **JOSH WHITEMAN**

ILLUSTRATIONS BY **WILL VINK**

NOT FOR
ANKLE
BITERS

Welcome to Sydney – the 'Emerald City',

With the world's nicest harbour, it's really quite pretty.

The surface is gorgeous but give it a scratch,

And you'll see how the upsides all come with a catch . . .

The traffic's a shocker, we're awful at manners,

Cost of living's obscene and we've got no town planners.

Our pollies are crooks, the trains are all late,

And everything's metered in our nanny state.

But our apathy means we ignore our town's crimes

'Til they're spelled out for everyone in snarky rhymes!

So here's our A to Z, which we hope you'll find witty,

'Cos although we love Sydney, it can be a bit . . . shitty.

A is for apathy – we give zero fucks

That we're wrapped in red tape and a coffee's six bucks.

You'd think we'd rise up since it's all so unfair,

But all that's revolting is how little we care.

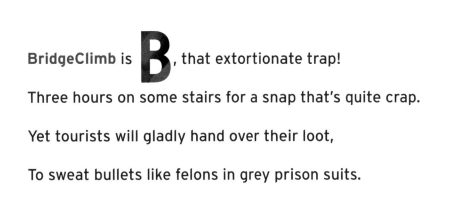

BridgeClimb is **B**, that extortionate trap!

Three hours on some stairs for a snap that's quite crap.

Yet tourists will gladly hand over their loot,

To sweat bullets like felons in grey prison suits.

C is cocaine, Sydney's favourite narcotic.

Keeps housewives amused and footballers psychotic.

400 a bag and we just can't say no,

It's Sydney's own version of playing in snow.

Darling Harbour's no darling of urban design,

Just a concrete homage to the year '89.

Now a cultural wasteland where corporates herd,

Forty licks of fresh paint couldn't polish this turd.

Eastern suburbs is **E** with its obscene incomes,

Home to Botoxed influencers and anti-vax mums.

Nouveaux riches come from far and will pay a top price

To live amongst arseholes . . . but Watsons Bay's nice!

New Year's Eve **F**ireworks - the big bang of the year.

Sky lights up! Crowd goes wild! And dogs shit with fear.

Then once the fun's done you're trapped on Bennelong Point,

It'll take 'til Jan 2 to get back to your joint.

The **G**adigal are Sydney's first daughters and sons.

They were fine 'til the Poms came with smallpox and guns.

Sure, we've said sorry for that act of aggression,

But a treaty? 'Yeah, nah. That's just out of the question.'

Homebush is **H** - we traipse out there like cattle,

To scream blue at the ref as we watch our team battle.

If we win then we grin and punch fists in the air,

Then it hits us: we're still stuck in bumfuck nowhere.

ICAC is ▮ – sounds like taking a poo,

And that isn't far off, with the work that they do.

The top end of town sure love fraud, graft and theft.

It's a wonder we have any government left!

James Cook is our **J**, the Elvis of our story.

Others came first but the white guy gets the glory.

He didn't discover Sydney – just parked in Botany Bay,

Drew some maps, had a swim, then pissed off on his way.

Ku-ring-gai Chase, our huge national park,

Goes off like a bunger from one little spark.

Each year some prick firebug keeps us on our toes:

Five million ready with a bucket and hose.

Lockout laws are our **L**, a nanny state tactic

To make every night out wholly anticlimactic.

Politicians double down on voter contempt,

As they proudly declare the casino exempt.

M's **mortgage stress** and it's all pretty bleak,

Wracking our brains how we'll pay for next week.

You work yourself silly for some wood, bricks and grass

But miss one repayment and you're out on your arse.

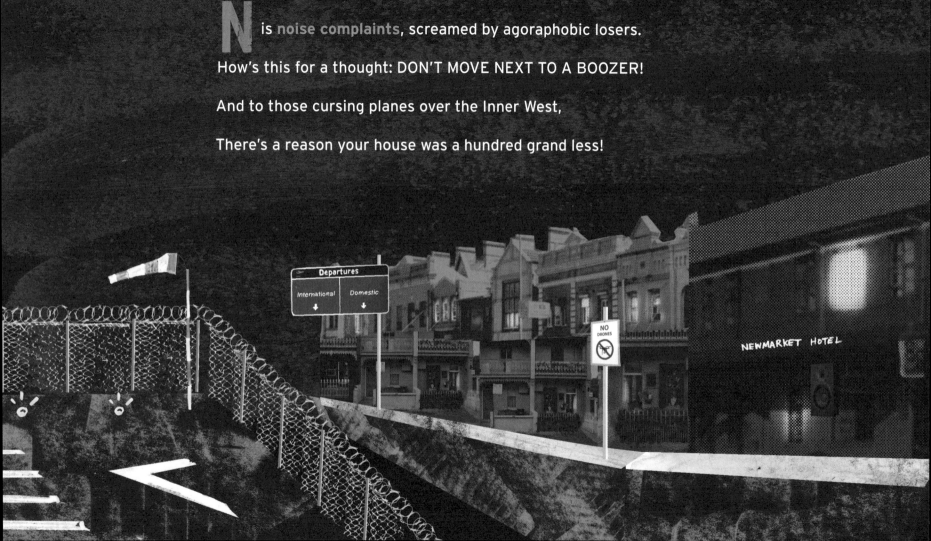

N is **noise complaints**, screamed by agoraphobic losers.

How's this for a thought: DON'T MOVE NEXT TO A BOOZER!

And to those cursing planes over the Inner West,

There's a reason your house was a hundred grand less!

O, our **Opera House** – greatest building of all!

Who cares if the sound's shit, the theatres too small?

Jørn Utzon was blackballed, his project derailed,

Now today's bureaucrats put the sails up for sale.

Wallets at the ready! **Parking fines** are our 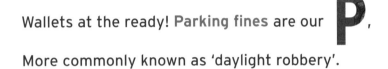P,

More commonly known as 'daylight robbery'.

Grey Ghosts and Brown Bombers we nickname these leeches,

Bleeding us dry from the hills to the beaches.

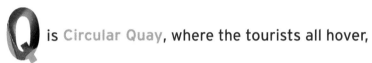 is Circular Quay, where the tourists all hover,

Screaming buskers, shitting seagulls – don't know why they bother.

Hit the Cahill Expressway – the view'll knock you dead.

(If not, then the car fumes will kill you instead.)

R's the **Royal Easter Show**, a family-fun winner,

Feed some piggies and a pony, pat a lamb before it's dinner.

Cough up fifty bucks for a showbag worth two,

Go broke on Coke and Pluto pups, then take home someone's flu.

Private or public? Who's in and who's out?

Yep, S is for schools – they're all we talk about.

'Odette's at Loreto.' 'Well, Auden's at King's.'

'My son's at the local.' 'Oh, that poor little thing!'

Traffic is **T** - it's the reason we're late,

Giant cars spitting smog while the drivers spew hate.

Turramurra Tractors in a hurry to pass,

Delivering organs? Nup, just kids to dance class.

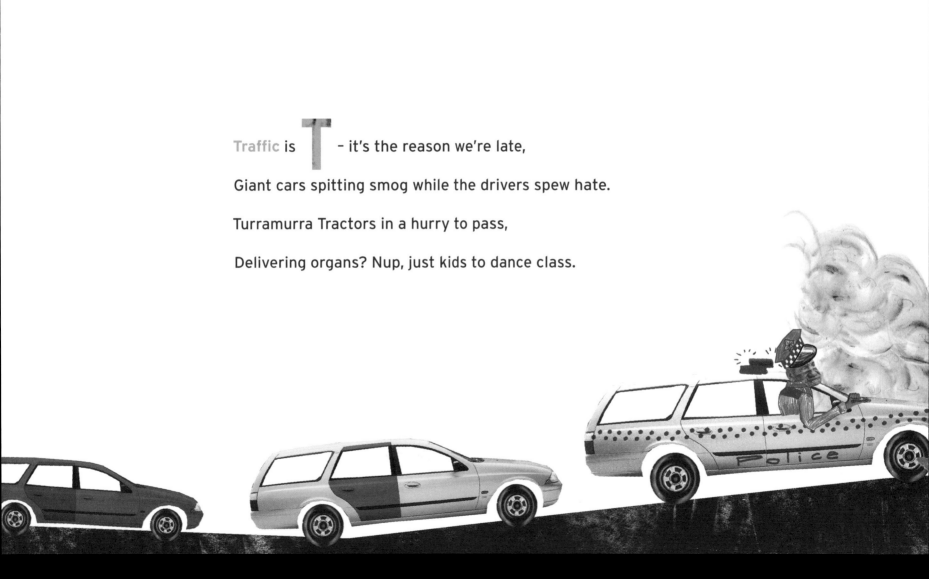

U is for ugg stores, there's five on each street.

Just how many peeps need sheep wrapped round their feet?

Past 10pm we're banned from buying more wine,

But want some wool boots? Sure, that's fine – join the line.

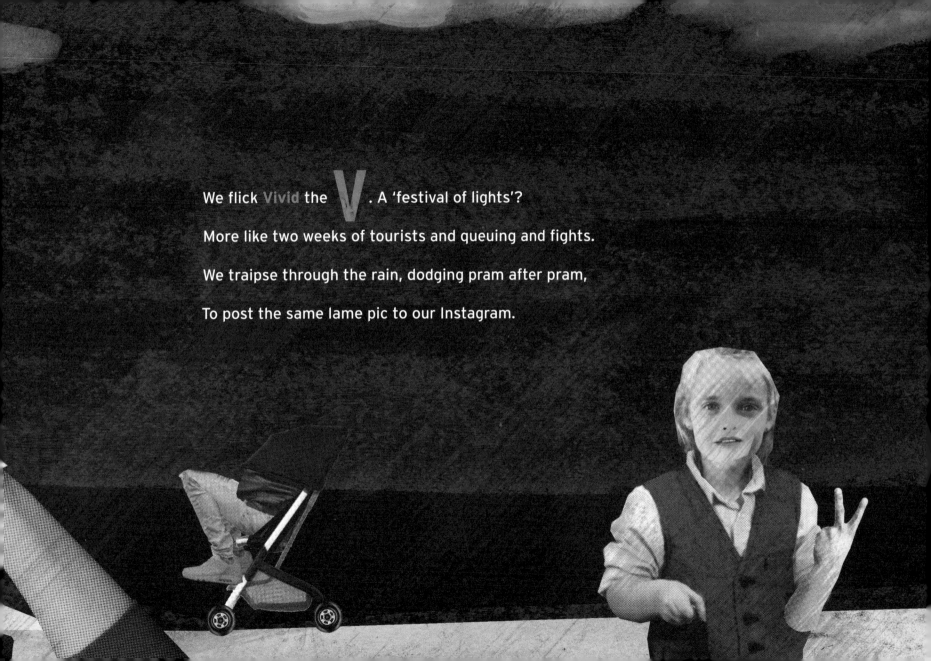

We flick Vivid the V. A 'festival of lights'?

More like two weeks of tourists and queuing and fights.

We traipse through the rain, dodging pram after pram,

To post the same lame pic to our Instagram.

We hate **W**et 'n' Wild but the kids think it's 'Wow!'

Trudge to Eastern Creek? Oh God, shoot me now.

Faced with slip-sliding Westies, Gen-X understand

This place ain't got nothin' on old **W**onderland.

X-rated is what our Kings X used to be:

Junkies and strippers, the smell of stale wee . . .

Then developers moved in with money to burn,

Now if you want a hooker, it's a trip to Redfern.

Yoga teachers are **Y** and in Sydney they're rife,

Study Bikram for an hour, you're a guru for life.

Sick of your day job? Lost your spiritual way?

Whack on your lululemons and have a 'Namaste.'

We've been whining since A, but we're **zealots** by Z :

Fanatics for Sydney from our hearts to our heads.

We tolerate a town that makes us want to self-destruct,

'Cos where else could we live? In Melbourne? Get fucked.

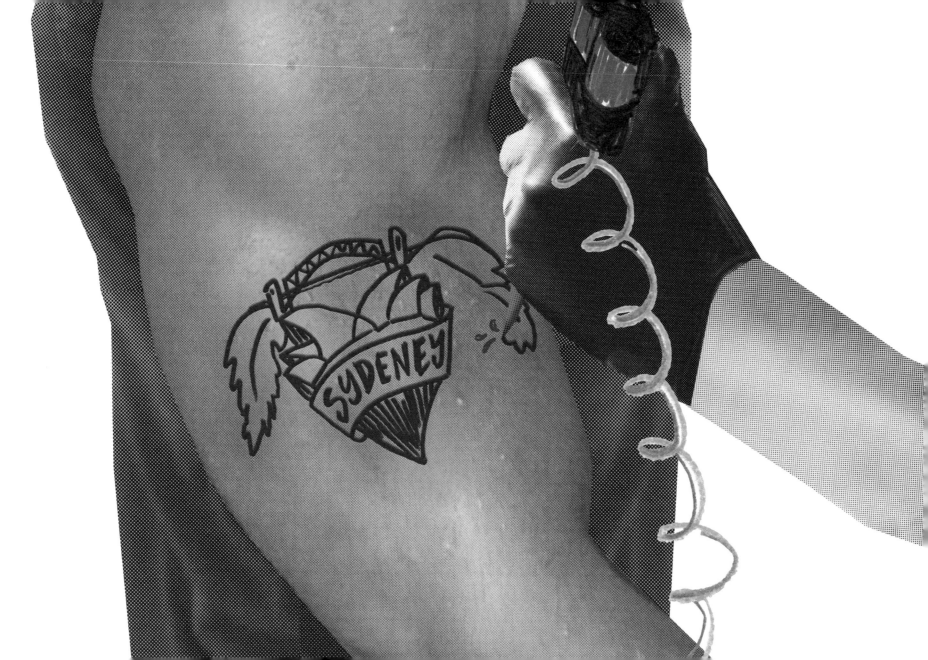

PENGUIN BOOKS

UK | USA | Canada | Ireland | Australia
India | New Zealand | South Africa | China

Penguin Books is part of the Penguin Random House group of companies whose addresses can
be found at global.penguinrandomhouse.com.

First published by Penguin Books, 2019

Cover and internal illustrations by Will Vink
Cover design by Adam Laszczuk © Penguin Random House Australia Pty Ltd
Internal design and typesetting by Adam Laszczuk

Printed and bound in China by RR Donnelley Asia Printing Solutions Limited

 A catalogue record for this
book is available from the
National Library of Australia

ISBN 978 1 76089 279 1

penguin.com.au

Paul Chappell and Josh Whiteman are the founders of Brand+Story,

a Sydney-based creative partnership. They both live in Sydney

with their families and enjoy nothing more than complaining

about living in the best city in the world.